EVERYDAY SCIENCE

Electricity

Please visit our web site at: www.garethstevens.com
For a free color catalog describing Gareth Stevens Publishing's list of high-quality books
and multimedia programs, call 1-800-542-2595 or fax your request to (414) 332-3567.

Library of Congress Cataloging-In-Publication Data

Riley, Peter D.
        Electricity / by Peter Riley. — North American ed.
            p. cm. — (Everyday science)
        Summary: Introduces electricity and circuits, as well as some of the electrical devices
    that are found in the home, such as refrigerators, CD players, and hair dryers.
        Includes bibliographical references and index.
        ISBN 0-8368-3247-7 (lib. bdg.)
        1. Electricity—Juvenile literature. [1. Electricity.] I. Title.
    QC527.2.R54   2002
    537—dc21   2002022633

This North American edition first published in 2002 by
Gareth Stevens Publishing
A World Almanac Education Group Company
330 West Olive Street, Suite 100
Milwaukee, Wisconsin 53212 USA

Original text © 2001 by Peter Riley. Images © 2001 by Franklin Watts.
First published in 2001 by Franklin Watts, 96 Leonard Street, London, EC2A 4XD, England.
This U.S. edition © 2002 by Gareth Stevens, Inc.

Series Editor: Rachel Cooke
Designers: Jason Anscomb, Michael Leamen Design Partnership
Photography: Ray Moller (unless otherwise credited)
Gareth Stevens Editor: Mary Dykstra

Picture Credits: iMac, courtesy of Apple Computers UK, p. 6; Pictor International, p. 22 (tl and br); Diane Laska-Swanke, electrical outlets,
pp. 6, 7, 23.

The original publisher thanks the following children for modeling for this book: Olivia Al-Adwani, Ammar Duffus, Russell Langer,
Gabrielle Locke, Rukaiyah Qazi, Giselle Quarrington, Perry Robinson, and Matthew Sharp.

Printed in Hong Kong

1 2 3 4 5 6 7 8 9 06 05 04 03 02

EVERYDAY SCIENCE

Electricity

Buzz!

Written by Peter Riley

Gareth Stevens Publishing
A WORLD ALMANAC EDUCATION GROUP COMPANY

About This Book

Everyday Science is designed to encourage children to think about their everyday world in a scientific way, by examining cause and effect through close observation and discussing what they have seen. Here are some tips to help you get the most from **Electricity**.

• This book introduces the basic concepts of electricity and some of the vocabulary associated with it, such as circuits, motors, and switches, and it prepares children for more advanced learning about electricity.

• The dangers of electricity should be discussed. Warnings appear on pages 7, 22, and 23.

• All experiments should be done with electricity from batteries that can be used to power toys. The experiments on pages 12, 13, 14, and 15 can be done with simple materials under adult supervision.

• On pages 13 and 19, children are asked to predict the results of a particular action or activity. Be sure to discuss the reasons for any answers they give before turning the page. Remember, in most situations, our solution is only one of several possibilities. Set up other activities for the children and discuss possible outcomes.

• The circuits in this book have been laid out to show their components and connections clearly. As indicated by the question on page 15 and its answer on page 29, these pictures can be used as a starting point for drawing circuit diagrams.

Contents

Electricity

Electricity makes
things work, or run.

A Walkman
runs on electricity.

A computer
runs on electricity.

Some electricity comes from batteries.

Some electricity comes through wires.

Electricity can harm you! Be very careful when you use it.

Batteries

Take a close look at a battery.

It has a plus sign on one end and a minus sign on the other end.

A battery holder has plus and minus signs, too. When you put a battery in place, you should match the plus and minus signs.

This flashlight has
two batteries.

You must put the plus sign of
one battery next to the minus
sign of the other battery to
make the flashlight work.

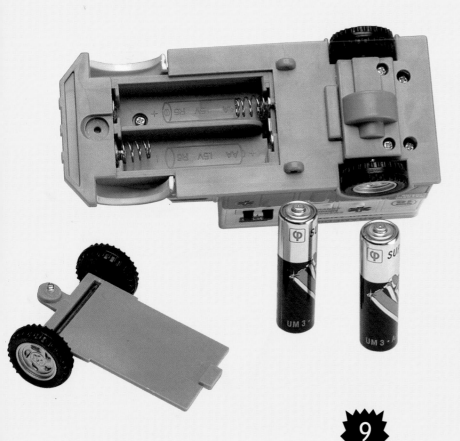

Find a toy that
uses batteries
and take out
the batteries.
Can you put
them back
in again?

What helps
you put them
back in?

Switches

This flashlight has batteries in it, but it is not lit up.

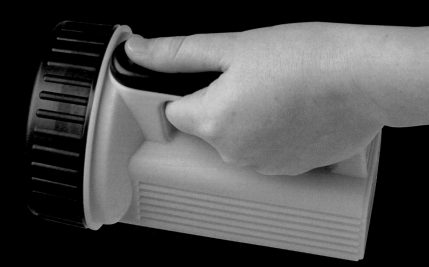

You use a switch to turn electricity on and off.

switch

You press the switch to make the flashlight work.

Toys that use batteries have switches, too.

On this toy, you slide the switch one way to make it work and the other way to make it stop.

on

off

What other kinds of switches do you use?

Make a **Circuit**

Electricity moves, or flows, in a circle called a circuit.

Make a circuit using a battery in a holder, a bulb, three wires, and a switch.

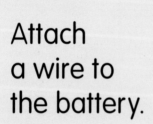

Attach a wire to the battery.

Attach the bulb to this wire.

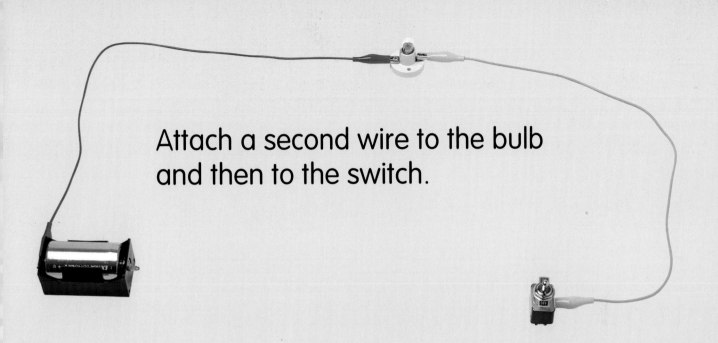

Attach a second wire to the bulb
and then to the switch.

Finally, use the third wire to attach
the switch to the battery.

What will happen when
you turn on the switch?
Turn the page to find out.

When you turn on the switch,
electricity flows through the wires,
and the bulb lights up.

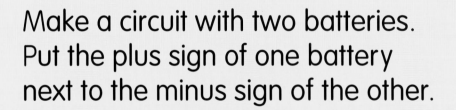

Make a circuit with two batteries.
Put the plus sign of one battery
next to the minus sign of the other.

Turn on the switch
and watch the bulb light up.

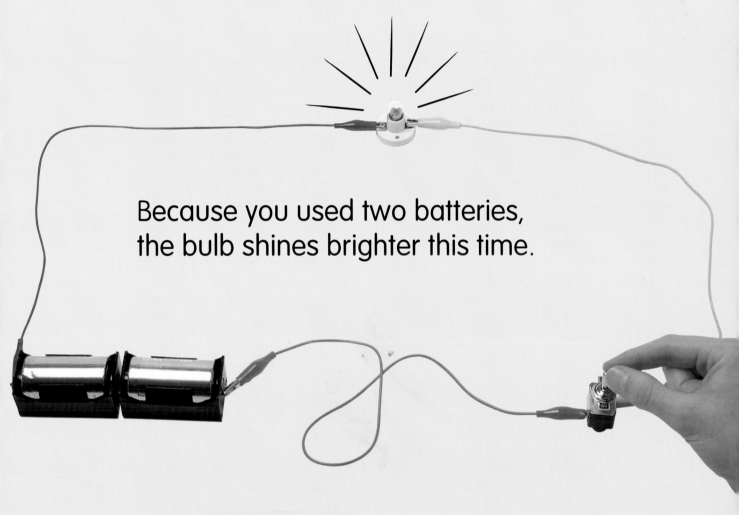

Because you used two batteries,
the bulb shines brighter this time.

More electricity is moving through the wires.

Make more circuits.
How can you record what you did?

Motors

When electricity flows through an electric motor, the motor's shaft turns.

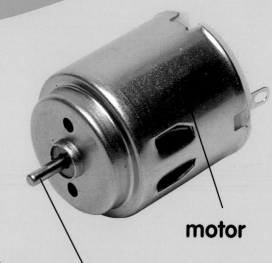

motor

shaft

An electric motor makes this toy boat's propeller spin.

Buzzers

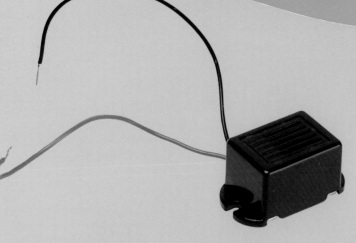

When electricity flows through a buzzer, the buzzer makes a sound.

Some toys have buzzers in them.
This toy ambulance has a loud buzzer.

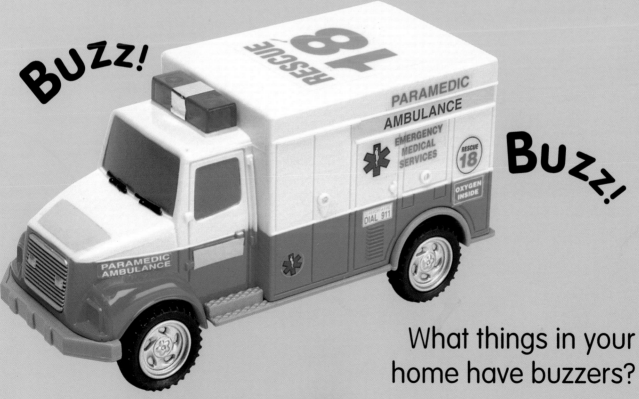

Buzz!

Buzz!

What things in your home have buzzers?

More Circuits

Kate made a circuit with a motor.

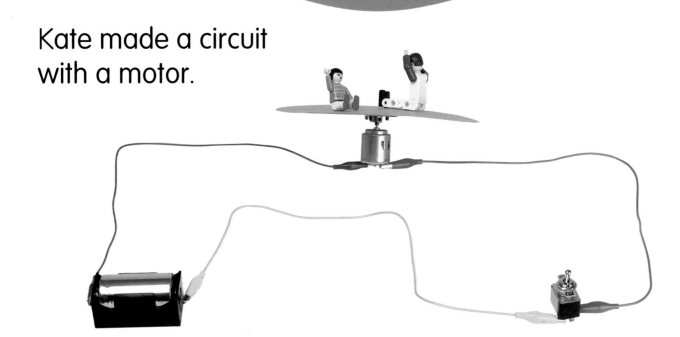

She put a propeller on the motor's shaft.

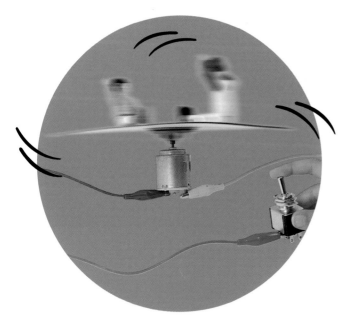

When Kate turns on the switch, the propeller spins.

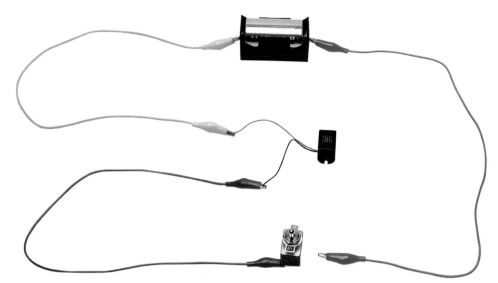

Paul made a circuit with a buzzer.

He wants to make Kate jump when he turns on the switch.

What do you think will happen?
Turn the page to find out.

Make It Work

Paul's buzzer did not work.

There is a gap in the circuit next to the switch.

The gap stops the electricity from flowing around the circuit.

Paul attaches the
wire to the switch
and turns on the switch.

This time
Kate jumps!

Buzz!

Make circuits with batteries and buzzers.
Why should you check them for gaps?

Making Electricity

Some electricity is made in power plants.

It flows through overhead cables.

It flows through substations into towns.

Electricity can be harmful. Keep away from cables and substations.

Inside a building, wires carry electricity to light switches.

Do not put your fingers into electrical sockets.

Wires also carry electricity to sockets.

Electricity flows through plugs and wires.

In the **Home**

toaster

Electricity can be used in many ways. It can make things hot, and it can make things cold. It can make light and sound, and it can make things move.

refrigerator

coffeepot

doorbell

hair dryer

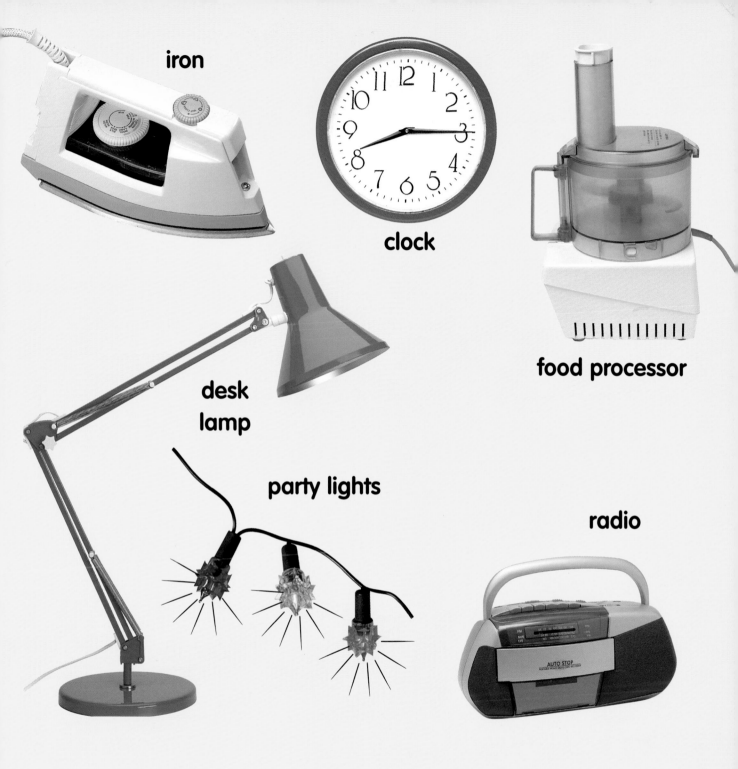

iron

clock

food processor

desk lamp

party lights

radio

Here are some objects in the home that use electricity. Why do they use electricity? Turn the page to find out.

Sort Them **Out**

The objects on pages 24 and 25 can be sorted into groups according to why they use electricity.

to make things hot

hair dryer   iron   toaster   coffeepot

to make things cold

refrigerator

to make light

party lights   desk lamp

to make sound

doorbell   radio

to make things move

clock   food processor

Here is a chart of these groups.

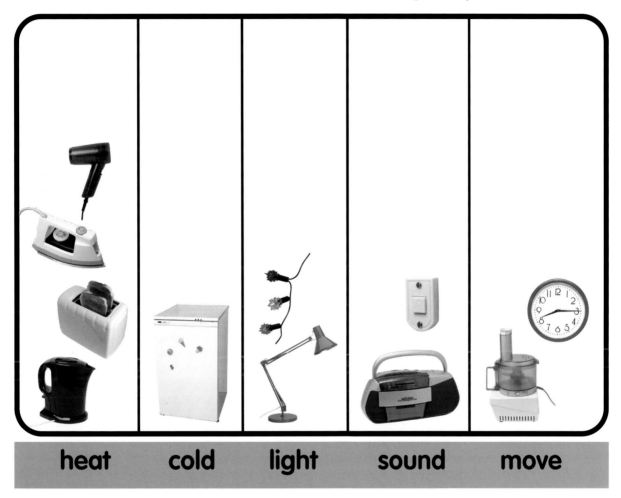

heat	cold	light	sound	move

Put the electrical objects in your home into groups like these and make a chart of the groups. Do any electrical objects fit into more than one group?

Useful Words

battery: a special cylinder or box that stores electricity. It can be used to make an electric circuit work.

buzzer: a device that makes a sound when electricity passes through it.

cable: a very thick wire that carries electricity from place to place.

circuit: a complete circle around which electricity flows.

gap: a break in a circuit that stops the flow of electricity.

motor: a device that makes something move when electricity passes through it.

plug: a piece that is found on the end of a wire. It fits into a socket to make electrical objects run.

power plant: a place where electricity is made and carried by cables to substations.

substation: a place where electricity moves from a thick cable to smaller cables that will carry it into homes.

switch: a device that starts or stops the flow of electricity.

wire: a thin piece of metal through which electricity flows.

Here are some answers to the questions asked in this book. If you had different answers, you may be right, too. Talk over your answers with other people and see if you can explain why they are right.

page 9   The plus and minus signs on the batteries and inside the toy help you put the batteries back in place.

page 11   There are lots of different switches. Some, such as a light switch, you push, and some, such as the switch on a radio, you twist.

page 15   You can write down what happened, but a quick and easy way to record circuits is to draw them. Here are two drawings of a circuit:

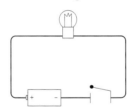 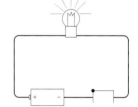

page 17   Some examples of things in the home with buzzers inside them are clocks, smoke alarms, and doorbells.

page 21   You should check for gaps because electricity will not flow if there is a gap in the circuit.

page 27   A toaster also moves when it pops up. Some refrigerators also have a light inside. Some clocks also make a sound. Lamps also give out heat. A hair dryer also has a motor inside that moves a fan.

For More Information

More Books to Read

- *All About Electricity. Do-it-Yourself Science* (series)
  Melvin Berger
  (Econo-Clad Books)

- *Electricity. Simply Science* (series)
  Darlene R. Stille
  (Compass Point Books)

- *Science Factory: Electricity and Batteries*
  Michael Flaherty
  (Copper Beech Books)

Web Sites

- BrainPOP: Where Does Electricity Come From?
  www.brainpop.com/science/electricity

- Edison International Kids Power Lab
  www.edisonkids.com

Index